Helping Children See Jesus

ISBN: 978-1-933206-03-5

Ly Huy's Escape
A Story of Vietnam

Author: Rose-Mae Carvin
Review Questions: Bryan Willoughby
Artist: Alice M. Turner
Computer Graphic Artists: Ed Olson, Yuko Willoughby
Page Layout: Kelley Moore (pointsandpicas.com)

© 2017 Bible Visuals International
PO Box 153, Akron, PA 17501-0153
Phone: (717) 859-1131
www.biblevisuals.org

All rights reserved. No part of this publication may be reproduced, stored in a retrieval system or transmitted in any form by any means, electronic, mechanical, photocopy, recording or otherwise, without the prior permission of the publisher, except as provided by USA copyright law.

LY HUY'S ESCAPE
Author: Rose-Mae Carvin

For a group-setting format of this story and other related items, please visit our web store at shop.biblevisuals.org and search using "5275".

CHAPTER 1

Ly Huy slept restlessly on his mat of straw.

It was not the hard floor of dried mud on which his mat was spread that made him restless. Neither was it the sound of war nearby. To these he long had been accustomed. Usually Huy slept soundly as do most nine-year-old boys. But it was Huy's dream which disturbed him. In the dream he seemed to hear again the voices of village children. They told of listening to two strange ladies.

One, they said, was a pale woman with yellow hair and blue eyes who spoke a foreign language. With her was a Vietnamese lady who showed them a black Book which told about a foreign God and how to get to Heaven.

In his dream Huy heard the boys and girls say, "The Book is magic. Our Buddhist priest said so. With this Book the pale lady gets boys and girls to go to the big city. There they take out the dark eyes of our Vietnamese children and send them to those of another land who have only blue eyes. Our priest says we must not listen to her. If we do, Buddha will be furious. Our priest made both women leave our village. He said, "The Vietnamese woman is under the spell of the light-skinned lady. Beware of the pale woman!"

Little Kim was not disturbed by dreams. She had learned, even as a baby, that her brother Huy always took good care of her. She felt safe when he was near. So she slept soundly on her mat next to him. Their mother and father slept close by in their one-room thatch-roofed home.

Huy felt someone shaking him awake. In the darkness he could not see who it was. Frightened, he sprang to his feet. *Have I been dreaming?* he wondered. *Or has the pale lady come to take me away?*

His mother's soft voice soothed him. "Don't be afraid, my son," she whispered. "It is only that the guns are getting closer. Your father says we must escape. Shh! We must not waken Kim!"

Huy could barely see the shadowy figure of his mother as she felt her way around. Still whispering, she said, "I have packed a bundle with some clothing and food. You are to carry Kim and this stick. Your father will lead the pig. But if it gets lazy you poke it with the stick. Make him walk fast. We must hurry before the soldiers get here."

Huy was wide awake now. He heard the pig grunt as his father tied a rope around its body.

They were on their way. On their way to where? No one knew exactly. Not even Father. He knew only that he must get his family beyond range of those guns. He was terrified of the enemy soldiers—terrified of what might happen to him and his family.

They hurried on in the darkness. Huy's mother balanced the food bundle on her head. Carefully she carried the little image of Buddha wrapped in cloth. To let it fall would surely displease the gods and perhaps bring worse disaster to her family.

Huy toted the sleeping Kim on his hip. In the other hand he held the stick which he had to use often on the pig. The pig did not like being tied with rope. Nor did he want to be pulled and prodded. Indeed, the pig did not like having to move. So he voiced his displeasure with loud grunts.

They trudged a long, long time before the sun began to rise. Then the father said, "We must look for a place to hide."

The rice field looked inviting. At the water's edge they settled down wearily. Lying there, Huy could see some water buffalo. He watched the herons (birds) picking and eating snails and small fish. He thought, *Those buffalo and herons are friendly to each other. Why can't people be like that instead of fighting?*

That night–and for many nights–the family plodded along under cover of darkness. They took shelter near a rice field or in an abandoned hut before the sun began to rise. It was not safe to travel by day, for they would be spotted by airplanes. "They will drop a bomb on anything that moves," the father warned.

When they found a hut to stay in, Huy's mother managed to make a tiny fire–just big enough to boil some rice. She knew the firelight might let the enemy know where they were. "But," she said, "it is less dangerous than risking a fire out-of-doors where it surely would be spotted by planes."

The mother boiled as much rice as she could, fed the family, and put some in a sack to be saved for the next day–and perhaps the next. After eating their rice, they spread their mats and slept until nightfall. Then they started out again. By now they knew they were headed toward a big city where they hoped to find safety.

Often they heard news through others who were also fleeing from their homes. One boy, Huy's age, carried a year-old brother. His parents had been torn from him. He whispered to Huy, "When we get to the river, I'll get somebody to tie my brother on my back, and we'll swim to safety. We'll never again have to be afraid of these soldiers." Huy was glad his father was a good swimmer. He'd take care of Kim.

One morning, early, as Huy and his family were eating their rice, they heard voices outside the hut–men's voices. One said, "Our search team went through this village and we know it was deserted. But last night a scout reported seeing some families traveling this way. He said one family has a pig."

"Let's find them! Even thinking of a pig dinner makes me hungry." Both men laughed as they walked near the tiny hut where Huy and his family were hiding.

Quickly Huy picked up his little sister. Holding her tightly in his arms, he crouched low in a corner. Kim looked up at him, frightened. "Don't be afraid, little sister," Huy whispered. "I'll protect you. I'll never, never leave you–never!" Huy rocked Kim in his arms, whispering as he did so, "Na, na, na. Don't cry. The soldiers will hear you."

Huy saw his father tiptoe toward his mother, standing in front of her to protect her. All were breathless and perfectly quiet–all but the pig. "Oink, oink," it grunted.

The family was petrified. Outside a Communist soldier called, "Did I hear a pig grunt?"

"Yes!" the other answered. "I think it came from inside that hut. Let's get it!"

The soldiers, stooping low, rushed into the hut. Blinking, one exclaimed, "Well! What have we here? Something more than a pig, I see!"

Both soldiers grabbed Huy's father. Dragging him outside one demanded, "What are you doing here?" Without waiting for an answer, he continued, "You work for the government," pointing his rifle at the poor man.

A shot rang out and Huy stole to the opening of the hut, peeking outside. There lay his father . . . dead!

Before the soldiers turned again toward the hut, Huy rushed to the corner to protect Kim. His mother handed the Buddha to him. Then, turning slowly, she swayed a little, fainted and fell quietly in a heap.

Huy made no sound. But he shuddered and broke out in a cold sweat as he saw one of the soldiers carry his mother outside. The other soldier dragged the pig. Huy heard one say, "Well, we got quite a loot! A pig and a woman." Both men laughed–loud, harsh laughter.

Huy watched his mother and the pig being dragged away, until he could see them no longer.

Sadly he turned to little Kim and fed her some rice. He could eat nothing. The lump in his throat was in the way.

Huy knew it would be safer to stay inside than go outdoors. He felt sure the soldiers had no interest in him nor Kim who was now sound asleep. Exhausted, Huy curled up on the straw mat beside his little sister. From time to time Kim whimpered in her sleep. When Huy put his arm over her, she became quiet. In her light sleep she sensed he was taking care of her. The bursting bombs and zooming jets didn't disturb her at all.

Huy thought, *I shall never let anyone take Kim away from me. Never! Never!* Much later, he finally dozed off.

Both children slept the rest of the day and into the night. When they awoke, Huy's first thoughts were of his father and mother and the terrible things which had happened. His next thought was, *We should have been on our way hours ago.* He scooped up the rice his mother had prepared, offered some to his idol, Buddha, and thinned out some for Kim. He himself ate a tiny portion, thinking, *I am responsible for Kim. I wonder where my mother is. Oh, why did they kill my father? I must be a man. But can I? Yes! I must! I shall!*

Doing as his father had done, Huy followed others who were fleeing for safety. All moved cautiously and only at night. During the daylight hours both children slept in some hiding place.

Each day he thinned out the rice a bit more for Kim. Each day he ate less and less himself. And each day as he carried his little sister, she felt lighter than before. *What would Mother do if she were here?* he wondered. *Oh, what did those soldiers do to her?*

Huy dragged on wearily toward the big city. He was certain he'd find food there.

And find food he did, in the big city. But it was food he begged, stole, or found in garbage cans. He went on the street only at night. By day he and Kim slept in alleys or dumps. Their clothing became ragged and filthy. And they were very, very hungry. Yet always he offered a part of their food to the idol, Buddha.

One night Huy ventured out a bit earlier than usual. He knew he had to find food or they would both die. He was so weak he could scarcely carry his wee sister. *If only she were old enough to walk just a little*, he thought, and was immediately ashamed of himself. Even if she were old enough she was too weak to take one step.

Where is my mother? What happened to her? he thought anxiously. Remembering his idol, he said, "Buddha, why don't you help us? Every day I give you some of the food we need. But you do not help. Why?"

CHAPTER 2

Huy trudged wearily along the narrow, dirty streets, darting into the deeper shadows whenever anyone passed.

It was getting dark quickly now. Suddenly he saw two women—one with light hair. She was taller than the other, a dark-haired Vietnamese lady. Huy strained his eyes to see. It was . . . yes, it was the fair-skinned woman with yellow hair and blue eyes whom the boys and girls of his village had described.

He slunk into the darkest corner he could find, trembling and nearly dropping his ailing, sleeping sister. Tightening his arms about Kim, he made himself as flat as he could against the wall. After a while, he crept out in the darkness to see if the women had gone. As he did so, he bumped into the Vietnamese lady.

Huy did not guess that the God the woman loved and served had caused her to turn back to the narrow street. He knew nothing of the God of love who could make His will known to His followers.

The Vietnamese lady held out her arms. "Hello. How are you?" she said softly. "My name is Lan. You may call me Co Hai." Huy, unafraid, went to her. Her arms—warm and protecting—made him think of his mother. *If only my mother were here*, he thought. And then he saw the light-haired woman. Frightened, he tried to struggle out of Co Hai's arms. She held him and little Kim who was crying weakly, close to her. Jerking her head over her shoulder, she signaled the other lady to leave.

"Stop trembling, boy," Co Hai said. "She has gone. She would do you no harm. But she understands that you are afraid of her. Now, come with me. I shall give you some good food and a place to sleep." Huy, weak from lack of food and rest, tried to struggle out of the woman's arms. The exertion was too much for him. He slumped, unconscious, to the ground.

When he regained consciousness, Huy did not know where he was. But as he opened his eyes he saw Co Hai's kind face. Somehow, he knew she was his friend.

The woman held a bowl of rice to his mouth. He grabbed it and began gulping. "No, boy. Take it slowly. You may have it all. But you must not eat it too fast."

Suddenly, Huy sat up straight, a frightened look on his face. "Where is Kim?" he asked. Co Hai pointed to a mat on the floor where the child was sleeping peacefully. "Kim has eaten some rice. She is going to be all right."

After he finished eating, Huy crawled toward his little sister and lay down at the edge of the mat. He put his arm over her and, almost immediately, was sound asleep.

Huy had no way of knowing that the light-haired woman of whom he was afraid was nearby. Indeed, he was sleeping in a large house which she used for children such as he. He did not know she was a missionary. Nor had he any way of knowing it was her strong arms which had carried him here. She had placed him tenderly in this room with the Vietnamese lady, away from other boys and girls.

The sun was high in the sky the next day when Huy opened his eyes. Half asleep, he realized something was wrong. Suddenly he knew what it was. Kim was not beside him. Jumping to his feet he began to call her name. Then he saw her. She was asleep in what looked like a cage. (Huy had never seen a crib before.) Kim had been bathed and was wearing clean clothing. *How beautiful she is!* Huy thought. He tried not to notice how dreadfully thin she was, as he stroked her straight black hair, smooth and shiny now since it had been washed. Then, suddenly he was terrified. Because his sister was in a cage, it must mean this Vietnamese lady planned to give Kim to that awful fair-skinned lady. She would ship her to another land where they would take out her lovely eyes. Perhaps they were already taken out! He had to know! He patted her and called, "Kim, Kim." When she opened those lovely dark eyes and held out her arms to him, he saw that, so far, she was all right. *But I must get her out of here*, he determined.

Quickly Huy snatched the blanket which had been covering Kim and wrapped her in it. He tiptoed to the door of the room. Just as he was about to open it, someone on the other side opened it.

There stood his friend of the night before—Co Hai. In her hands she held a bowl of soup, some rice and fish. Over her arm hung boy's clothing—clean and new. She closed the door and stood against it.

"Don't you understand, Huy, that I am your friend?" She spoke gently. "If you do not trust me, you may leave. I shall not stop you. But first, would you like to have a bath, some clean clothes, and food?"

Huy was not entirely sure he was doing the right thing. But the food smelled good—like his mother's. And a bath and clean clothing would be comfortable. In his heart he longed to stay close to this woman who reminded him of his mother. *Why, why, why did those men take my mother?* he wondered.

Behind a screen, in the corner of the room, Huy used a bowl of water, soap, and a long-handled brush. He stood in a small tub and scrubbed.

From time to time, Huy peeked around the screen to make certain Kim was still there. She was trying to catch a sunbeam which streamed through the window.

In time, Huy came from behind the screen, all shining clean and in new clothing. The woman said, "You are a fine-looking boy. But you'll look even better when you have eaten."

Huy slurped his soup, making the usual soup-eating noise to which he was accustomed. He began to eat the fish and rice. Suddenly he stopped. "I must offer some of this to Buddha," he explained. "Where is my Buddha?"

"Over there." The woman pointed to a corner of the room. She did not try to stop Huy as he set up the idol.

He knelt before the image, hands held together, and bowed low, head touching the floor. "Forgive me," he begged, "for not giving this to you before I ate. Now I bring you this offering, O Buddha." And he placed some rice and fish in the empty soup bowl and set it before the idol—a man-made god which could not see, nor feel, nor hear, nor eat.

"While you eat, Huy," Co Hai said, "I shall tell you something you must know. All that I say is true. The living God of Heaven loves you. It was He who caused you to bump into me on the street when it was almost too dark to see anything. We had prayed to Him before we went out. We asked Him to show us where to find some child who needed us. It was He who sent us to you."

Then, for the first time, Huy heard truths he had never known. The woman's face glowed as she told that God loves everyone—man, woman, and child. He loves them so much that He sent His only Son, the Lord Jesus Christ, to earth as a baby. When He grew to be a man, He taught great crowds and healed those who were sick.

"Huy, the Lord Jesus is not an ordinary man. He is the very Son of God. A man who was simply good could not do the wonders He did. Are you listening, Huy?" she asked, as the boy remained silent.

His mouth full of food, Huy nodded his head. He really did not want to listen. His keen mind was busily at work.

Co Hai had said "we" when she told about the God who had sent them to find some child needing help. We? Who was the other person? There had to be another. Although Co Hai was certainly strong, she could scarcely have carried him *and* Kim. Carry them where? What house was this to which he and Kim had been brought? Then came the frightening thought, *Was it the woman with yellow hair and blue eyes who helped carry us here? Is she hiding somewhere waiting to capture us?* He felt he could trust this lady who reminded him of his mother. Yet he would have to be on the lookout for the other one. Then, for a time, at least, Huy forgot his fear and listened.

He listened eagerly now as the woman said, "God's Son, the Lord Jesus Christ, loves all people so much that He was willing to be nailed to a cross and die for us who are sinners. God accepted His sacrifice and raised Him from the dead. Now all who will place their trust in Him can have their sins forgiven. They can know that when they die they will be safe in Heaven with Him—forever. When our trust is in the Lord Jesus, we receive His kind of life—everlasting life. This is a marvelous gift, Huy, and God wants you to have it."

Although Huy did not quite understand, he felt something stirring in his heart. He had no way of knowing it was the Holy Spirit of God speaking to him. How could he? He had never heard about the Holy Spirit. He never heard about the God who loves all people everywhere. Huy sat quietly when the lady stopped speaking. Then she held up her black Book and said, "Huy, we know all of what I have been telling you is true because it is written here in God's Book." Huy was terrified. This was the Book of magic about which his friends in the village warned him. He had been trapped! He must not stay in this house!

Abruptly, Huy got to his feet, snatched his little sister, grabbed Buddha his idol, and hurried toward the door. This time the woman did not try to stop him, though she did not understand why her Bible frightened him. But then she had no way of knowing that he had been told it was a book of magic. And she did not know about Huy's awful dream the night he and his parents had to leave their home.

"You do not need to run, Huy," she said. "No one will stop you. But remember this! If you really love your sister you will bring her back here. I hope you do so before she dies—for die she surely will—unless she gets better care than you can give her. Are you determined to go?"

Huy stopped at the door. "Yes, I am going. You have been kind. But I shall not stay and listen to stories of a strange God and have you use magic on us with that little Book."

There was a puzzled look on Co Hai's face as she watched Huy turn and leave, Kim in his arms, the idol in his hand. Immediately she began praying that he would return and learn to know the true and living God who could cast out all his fear.

CHAPTER 3

It was beginning to get dark as Huy fled from the Christian Home for Children. He tried to keep out of sight as much as possible for he knew the lovely, clean clothing he and Kim were wearing might be stolen from them.

Once more Huy was begging food, getting it from garbage cans, or stealing it. Always he thought about and wished for his mother. Before many days their clothing had become dirty and torn. Again they were always hungry and afraid.

Often Huy sneaked to the children's home and watched the boys and girls playing in the yard. He observed how well and happy they were. Then he would look at his skinny little sister who was easier to carry each day because she was getting lighter and lighter.

If I take her to the home, he wondered, *will they care for her, now that I have run away? If they would, how can I give her up? No! This I cannot–will not–do!*

Huy determined to get more food for Kim–somehow. He did not know just how. But he could not leave her in a place where they worshiped a foreign God. Buddha would be angry if Kim began to worship any other God.

But what, really, is Buddha doing for us? Huy began to reason. *Surely not much. Buddha demands part of our little bit of food. But he gives us nothing. Can the foreign God be the real God after all?*

But, Buddha or no Buddha, foreign God or no foreign God, Huy could not–would not–give up his little sister whom he dearly loved. She could not die! She must not die! He would not let her die! Huy refused to believe what he saw–that little Kim could not live much longer. Her thin arms, no longer able to cling to him, hung limply at her side.

Over and over he sang to her, hoping to make her feel better:

> Lulla-lullaby, dear sister,
> Na-na, na-na, na.
> Lulla-lullaby, dear sister,
> Na-na, na-na, na.
> I shall care for you, dear sister,
> I shall never leave you.
> Lulla-lullaby, dear sister,
> Na-na, na-na, na.
> Na-na-na, na-na-na.

One day, about two weeks after Huy had left the Children's Home, he heard a soft, familiar voice. "Huy! Huy! I've found you at last. I have prayed that God would help me find you. I want to help you and Kim. Whether or not you allow her to live in the home, I want to help you. Please tell me what it was that frightened you into running away. What did I do to you?"

Once more, both Huy and Kim were being held in Co Hai's arms—arms which felt like his mother's. And she was crooning, "Na, na, na." Huy began sobbing out his story of fear of the light-haired woman and the little Book.

"Why did you not tell me this before, Huy?" Co Hai asked. "Please believe me. None of this is true. Listen, please. The foreign lady came to our land because she loves God very much. She wanted to obey Him. So when He put it into her heart to cross the ocean to Vietnam, she obeyed. She left her own mother and father, sisters and brothers, to come to a strange land. She does only good. Never does she harm boys and girls. Never, never would she take eyes from children to give to other children."

Putting her cheek against Huy's, now wet with tears, she said, "It makes me sad to hear what you have said about her, and to know the boys and girls in your village believe these lies. The little Book is not magic! It is made only of paper."

Taking a little Bible from the folds of her dress, Co Hai held it up. "This is the Word of God, Huy. It has no magic—*no magic*."

Huy stiffened, still afraid. Co Hai ignored this. She continued, "Huy, I have been your friend. Why did I try to find you? Because I have learned from reading this Book that God loves me. And He loves you. I love Him and want others to know about Him. Would you like to hear more from this Book which God has given us? You can learn to know and love this Book, which we call—not magic, Huy—oh no! Not magic, but it is God's Word, the Bible. Now we must take your little sister home so she can have the food and care she needs."

When Co Hai felt Huy pulling away from her she said, "Remember, without proper care, Kim cannot live long. Now before we go I want you to reach out your hand and touch this book, the Bible. Touch it! Touch it! As your friend, I promise nothing will harm you."

With trembling fingers Huy—wondering what his mother would think—reached out and gently touched the Bible. When nothing happened he smiled shyly at Co Hai, saying, "We are friends."

Without another word, the lovely Christian Vietnamese lady and the dirty, hungry boy walked together. Huy allowed her to carry Kim. In a low voice she crooned to the little girl, "Na, na, na."

When they reached the home, Huy and Kim were given the same loving care as before. They were permitted to sleep in a room away from the others, with Co Hai caring for them.

The next morning there was a gentle knock at the door. When the woman opened it, there stood the light-haired missionary, a smile on her beautiful face. She did not try to touch the children, knowing Huy's fear.

She was still smiling as she said, in Vietnamese, "I speak your language very poorly. But can you understand me?" Huy nodded his head. He was trembling a little. Not so, little Kim. She looked into the lady's face and tried to hold up her tiny, weak arms.

"She wants me to hold her," the woman said. "May I, Huy? I promise not to take her away from you."

Huy nodded. *This woman can't be bad*, he thought. *I'm sure Mother would like her. If only I knew where to find Mother.*

The days went by and Huy saw his little sister getting plump and happy. As her legs grew plump and strong, Kim began to walk. Huy knew he had made the right decision in coming to live in this home.

Now they both mingled with other children. However, at times, when Huy saw a child who was blind, he felt the old fear tugging again at his heart. But only for a moment or two.

Huy had come to understand some of the lessons in the Bible. He was certain now the Bible was not a book of magic, but did explain the love of God and His Son the Lord Jesus Christ. He had come to understand that God's Son died for him, as well as for everyone in all the world. He knew that to have salvation a person needed to believe and receive this Lord Jesus–the Saviour. Best of all, the day came when Huy truly believed that the Lord Jesus is the Son of God who died for *him*. He believed and received the Lord as *his* Saviour from sin.

The Bible had become an open book to him. He learned from it quickly and readily. He learned about Heaven with its streets of gold and other wonders. He understood, too, that there could be no sin in Heaven. Yet he, like everyone else, had been born with a sinful heart. He saw from the pages of God's Word that the Lord Jesus Christ, the Son of God, took upon Himself the sin of all the world. Because he, Huy, had placed his trust in Jesus the Saviour, his sins were forgiven. He had a clean, pure heart. He knew, too, from the Bible that he now had everlasting life. Like the trees that show by their green that they have life, he, too, had life–everlasting life. He would live forever in God's wonderful home, Heaven. He came to understand these truths and many others because the Holy Spirit who was now living in his heart, was his Teacher.

With a stronger body came a quick mind. So Huy learned the lessons he was taught. Because he had classes to attend and work to do, he was not always close to his sister. But he never allowed Kim to forget that she was indeed his sister. Each day they had a little playtime together when he told her simple truths of Jesus. Although she did not understand completely, Kim was thrilled to learn of the Saviour's love.

Then suddenly, fear again gripped Huy and those who cared for the children. Word came that the Communists were coming to take their city as they had the little villages. Day after day they could hear bombs bursting and war planes zooming overhead.

Huy knew only too well what this meant. He remembered the cruel Communist soldiers and what had happened to his father and mother the night the family was trapped inside the abandoned hut. What could he do? Should he take Kim and try to run away again and hide?

The Christian ladies knew what to do. They prayed. Many times they gathered the older children to pray with them. Huy learned to trust God for protection and care. Yet he was scarcely prepared for the day Co Hai led him to the office where the missionary sat at her desk.

Quietly the missionary said, "Huy, there is a decision you must make. A very important decision. It is about little Kim."

Huy thought: *Kim's eyes*. But only for a second.

Yet what the missionary said next seemed to make his heart stand still . . . turn topsy-turvy . . . tie itself into knots. She was saying, "Huy, you know we have prayed for God's protection." Huy made no sound. He kept his dark eyes on the missionary's face as she continued. "We believe," she said, "God has shown us what to do—what is best for our little ones." Huy stood silent. "There are some people in my country who will take our tiny ones and care for them, if we consent to let them go. We think Kim should go."

As Huy started to shout "NO!" she held up her hand for silence.

Continuing, she explained, "I have a sister in my homeland who has children of her own. She will gladly take Kim into her home and care for her. Kim will be part of the family there, if we allow her to go. The government here has consented to this."

"And I? May I go with her?" Huy's voice trembled.

There were tears in the missionary's eyes. "No, Huy," she replied. "The government will not permit boys your age to go."

"Then my sister cannot go! You have said I must make the decision." Drawing himself up to his full height and with dark eyes flashing, Huy repeated, "I say NO! I have said I shall never let her leave me. She cannot go!" Turning quickly, Huy started toward the door.

Co Hai, standing nearby, said, "Huy, if she stays here, do you know what may happen to her?"

Huy flashed her an angry glance and ran from the room. As Co Hai started after him the missionary said, "No, do not go. Let him fight this out on his own. Come, let us pray about it."

CHAPTER 4

Huy dashed to the street. He ran and ran until he could run no longer. Then he walked. Finally he stopped, gasping for breath, and slid to the ground to think. Later–much, much later–he turned and trudged toward the home. There he tiptoed inside so as not to be heard.

He flung himself on his sleeping mat. All night long he tossed and turned, fighting the battle of making another decision. This time he was not fighting alone. The Lord Jesus was now his Guide. And the Holy Spirit was speaking to him—speaking, trying to guide the boy.

By morning the battle was over. Huy had made his decision: *My sister must go where she will be safe–safe and well cared for. She will be loved. I love her too–love her enough to let her leave me.*

The love of the Lord Jesus in his heart helped him to give up his little sister. This was true, unselfish love.

Yet he wondered again and again, *What would Mother say about this? Oh, where is she? If only I could find her.* Almost every night he fell asleep, sobbing, "Mother, Mother."

Not many days later Huy stood and watched as Kim boarded a jet plane. Soon she would be in a quiet, peaceful land. Huy wondered what that would be like. Every day of his life, he had lived in a land of war.

Yet there was peace in the heart of this boy, now a Christian. It was the peace God alone gives in times of trouble and heartache. There was peace, but also a feeling of terrible, terrible loneliness as Huy gazed at Kim looking out the window waving at him. Then he turned away, not wanting to see the giant plane soar into the sky.

Huy went about his work and studies as usual. But he never smiled. He ate little. He slept little. *She will forget me*, he thought. *I shall never see her again. Soon she will not have one little thought for her brother. If only we could be together with Mother.*

A few weeks later Huy was called again to the missionary's office. He entered quietly and stood before her, head bowed.

The missionary was smiling. The smile was not only on her lips but seemed to be dancing about her eyes as she said, "We have some wonderful news for you, Huy." The excitement in her voice made Huy raise his eyes just as Co Hai entered the room. She also looked happy and excited.

The missionary continued, "I have asked Co Hai, who has been as a mother to you, to tell you the news."

Standing beside him Co Hai again put her arm around Huy. Once more he thought of his mother's arms. He held back the tears wondering, as before, *Where, oh where is my mother?*

Smiling happily, Co Hai asked, "Huy, how would you like to go to live in the land where your sister is?"

Huy looked at her with questioning eyes. "But boys my age are not permitted," he said, the hope creeping into his voice.

"This has been true," the lady answered. "But a small group of boys your age will be sent on a plane tomorrow. We have already made arrangements for you to join them."

Huy looked questioningly at the missionary. He was afraid to believe what she said. The thought came to him, *I shall only be disappointed if I hope for this. Besides, what would Mother say?*

The missionary, blue eyes shining with happiness, explained, "We do not understand the government's decision. But it is God's answer to our prayers." She waited for Huy to realize the truth of this. Then she added, "What makes all of us extra happy is that you will be living with Kim in my sister's home. And I have been asked to go along on the trip to take care of you and the other boys. You, Huy, will be with your sister—and I shall be with mine. I have not seen her for many years." Huy looked closely at the missionary now. He had never thought about her having a sister whom she missed. *How selfish I have been*, he thought. "Please, Lord, make me more unselfish," he prayed in his heart.

And so it was that Huy and the light-haired missionary were at the airport waiting to board the plane. Co Hai was there to see them off. Huy stood close beside her. "I wish you were going also," he said.

"But who would take care of the children who are still in the home? Do not worry about me, Huy. God will protect me. I shall pray for you always. Will you pray for me?"

Huy nodded yes. He did not dare to speak. He knew that if he did, the tears he was holding back could be held back no longer. Thoughts of his mother were almost too much for him.

As they stood there, many others nearby were also waiting for instructions. Huy paid no attention to them until he heard a familiar voice. His heart raced. He could not turn around for fear his ears had deceived him. Instead, he strained to hear what the voice was saying. His heart pounded harder as he heard the woman tell another, "My husband was killed and I was taken captive by some soldiers. I escaped and was sheltered by a kind family. Of course I am happy to have been chosen to help care for these children who are being flown to safety. But I shall return."

Huy trembled as he touched the arm of the missionary. Putting his finger across his lips he cupped his ear with his hand, signaling her to listen.

The familiar voice was saying, "You see, I have two children. After I was captured I never saw them. And I do not know what happened to them. I have searched and searched but have found no trace of them. So I shall come back as soon as I can. I must find them." The woman's voice broke as she continued, "My boy, Huy, is ten years old now, and my tiny girl, Kim, was only a baby when we were separated. I must find them! I must! I must!" she sobbed.

The missionary spun around to see who had been speaking. Not so, Huy. He stood absolutely still. He was afraid that what he hoped might not be true. He was trembling all over.

The missionary touched the woman's arm and pointed to Huy. The lady did not understand until the missionary, taking Huy by the shoulders, turned him around. Looking up, Huy saw the nicest, the kindest, the best face he had ever seen. "Mother?" he whispered.

They stood as they were for a moment—the woman and her son. Then with a little cry she drew him to her. With her arms about him he had no doubts. This surely was his own gentle mother.

CHAPTER 5

Orders rang out, "All boys for Flight Number Five, aboard!" There was no time for conversation. His mother had a question she dared not ask. But Huy understood. Turning from the ramp, he called, "Kim is all right. You'll see her."

Huy did not know which flight his mother would be on. Nor did he know her destination. Yet he knew that somehow the missionary would see to it that she would see Kim.

Then—wonder of wonders!—his mother, his very own mother, was told to board the same plane he was on.

The children all sat or lay on their mats on the jet cargo plane. As many as could pressed their noses against the windows watching the scenery below. When they were well out over the ocean, Huy was permitted to sit with his mother. Answering all her questions, he told her how he and Kim had scrounged for food before the two ladies took them in. He hesitated a bit when he told her that he no longer believed in Buddha. "Buddha did not help us, Mother," he explained. "It was the one true and living God who guided the missionary and the Vietnamese lady to Kim and me. He is the God of love. And He puts His love in the hearts of those who believe in Him. It was His love which made them care for us as they did, Mother."

Huy expected his mother to be angry. He remembered well how she had wrapped their family idol in cloth and warned him to take good care of it.

Instead of being cross, she smiled, saying, "My son, I, too, have come to know this true God. I have received His Son, the Lord Jesus Christ, into my heart. I learned about Him from the family who kindly took me in. It is indeed He who has brought us together." Huy thought his happy heart would burst.

They talked of other things, but mostly of Kim. His mother wanted to know all about her. Many times tears came to her dark eyes. Tears which she controlled and would not allow to fall. "If only she could know me—know that I am her mother," she said. "But she was too young."

Touching her hand, Huy said, "She will soon know you, Mother. She learns quickly."

Long hours later, a shout arose from the boys at the window. "We're here! We're here!" The plane slowly slipped down and came to rest in America–a strange land and "foreign" to Huy and the others. Inside the terminal they huddled close to each other in fear. Everything looked strange–the great building with its bright lights and all the white people scurrying about. The foreign smells and sounds were terrifying.

One by one the Vietnamese boys were turned over to friendly families who were eager to love and care for them. All the while Huy was stretching his neck this way and that, hoping to see the one he knew.

Suddenly he spied a tall blonde woman. This certainly must be the missionary's sister. In her arms she held a sleeping, dark-haired child. "Mother!" he shouted. "There is Kim! She's asleep!"

All eyes turned to the mother. With the missionary she squeezed through the crowd to the waiting sister. "This is Kim's mother," the missionary explained. Without a word her sister laid the sleeping child in the mother's arms. Her mother hugged Kim tenderly, saying, "Thank You, dear God. Thank You, dear God."

Little Kim stirred in the warm, loving arms. Opening her eyes, she looked up and smiled.

"She knows me! She knows me!" her mother sobbed.

Huy could wait no longer. Moving closer he called, "Kim!" For a moment, she looked puzzled.

Then she turned, trying to leap to him. He grabbed her and hugged her tightly. While he could not quite believe Kim remembered her mother, there was no doubt she remembered *him*.

As they walked to the waiting car, Huy thought, *I know Kim is smart. But she cannot possibly remember Mother. She was too little when Mother was taken from us.*

Suddenly he understood! It was the *feel* of his mother's arms. Kim had mistaken her for Co Hai whose gentle arms she remembered well. He knew how often those arms had comforted him.

But now they were with their mother—their very own mother! And they were safe.

That night Huy, his mother, and the missionary slept at her sister's home. He was in a room with two other boys. They slept on beds. But Huy had his very own mat on which to sleep. Too excited to close his eyes, he studied the boys sleeping on high bunks. He pulled his mat farther from the beds thinking, *Surely one of them will fall off while I'm asleep. There's nothing to keep them on those beds.*

Huy had much to think about. He thought of God and how good He was to bring his family together. He thought of the missionary. *Suppose she had never come to my country. She could have stayed here in this nice land with her family. She would have been far away from the war and fear which we have always known. How peaceful and quiet it is here! There are no zooming war planes. There's no noise of bursting bombs.*

Why had the missionary gone to Vietnam to care for children? Huy knew. The love of God in her heart made her love the people of his land. She loved the Lord enough to obey His command, "Go ye into all the world and preach the Gospel to every creature."

Before he slept that night Huy prayed, giving his life to God: "I, too, want to tell the Gospel of Your love, dear God. I want everyone to know that You love the world so much that You gave Your Son, the Lord Jesus Christ. And I'll tell them how Jesus, the perfect One, died, sacrificing Himself for the sins of the world. But I'll explain that He rose from the dead, lives now in Heaven, and someday–it may be soon–when Your trumpet will sound and Christ will come from Heaven for all who are His."

Then Huy promised, "I shall study hard in these strange American schools. And when I'm old enough I shall go wherever You want me to go, dear Lord. I, too, shall tell of You, the true and living God–the God of love and salvation. But between now and then I want to share this good news with all I meet right here in America."

After the "Amen," Huy slept peacefully with joy in his heart.

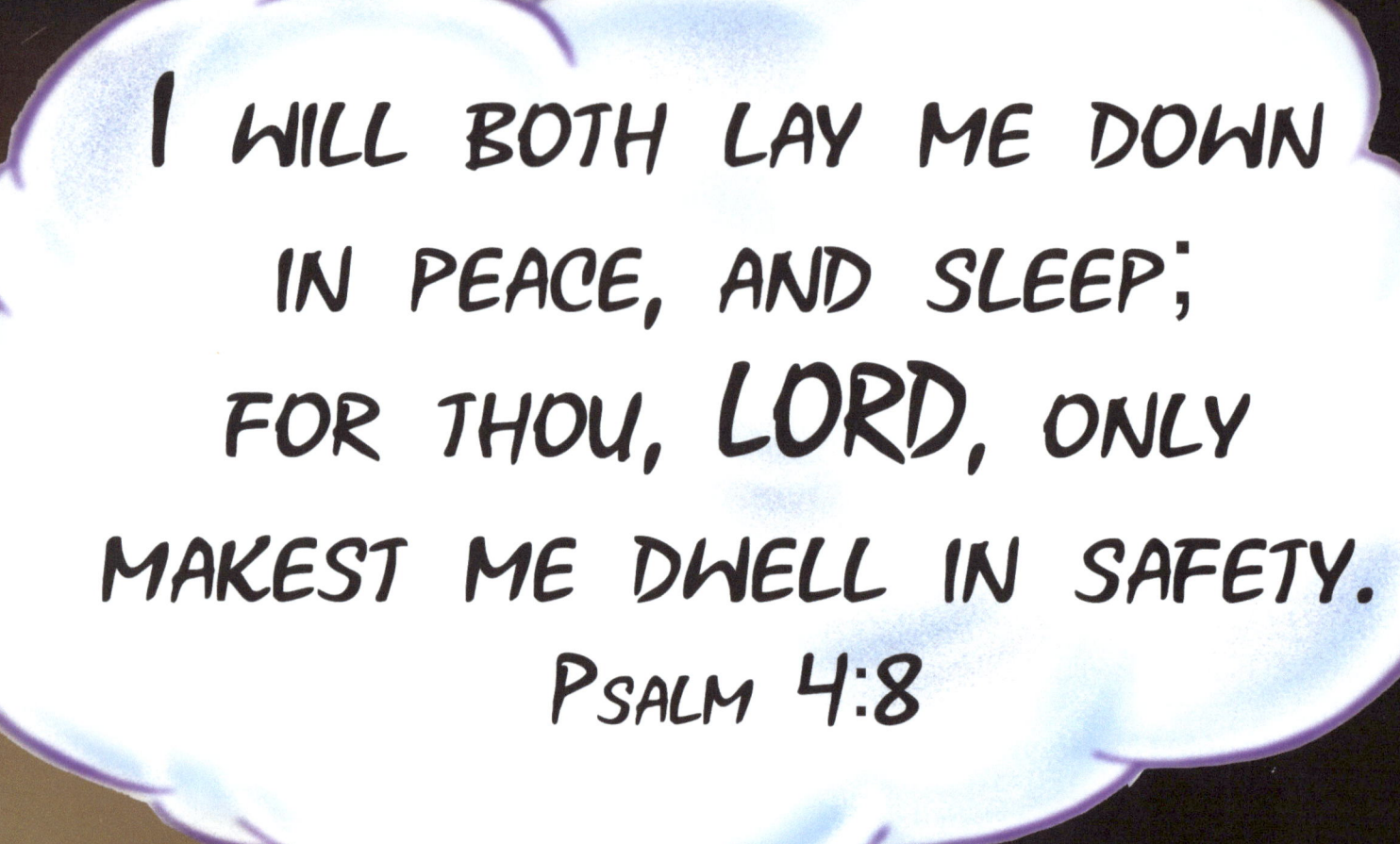

Review Questions

Chapter 1

1. How old was Huy? *(Nine years old)*
2. In his dream, Huy heard the voices of village children. What did those voices warn him about? *(The voices warned of a pale foreign woman and a Vietnamese woman with a magical black Book. The pale woman was said to take boys and girls to a big city where she would take out their dark eyes.)*
3. Why did Huy's mother wake him up in the middle of the night? *(The sound of gunfire was getting closer, and the family would need to escape.)*
4. What things did Huy's family take with them? *(A bundle of food and clothing, the pig, a stick for poking the pig, a little image of Buddha)*
5. Why did Huy's family travel only at night? *(The darkness kept them from being spotted by enemy airplanes.)*
6. What promise did Huy make to his little sister Kim? *(That he would protect her, and never leave her.)*
7. How did the two soldiers find Huy's family? *(They heard the pig grunting.)*
8. What did Huy's mother hand him before the soldiers carried her away? *(The Buddha)*
9. What words might you use to describe Huy and Kim's life in the big city? *(Miserable, scary, frustrating, hungry, lonely)*
10. When Huy was weak and hungry he said to the idol, "Buddha, why don't you help us?" If you were there listening, what would you say to Huy? *(That the Buddha cannot hear or help because it is not alive.)*

Chapter 2

1. How did Huy react when he spotted the two women? *(He was afraid and hid from them.)*

2. Who did Huy think about when the Vietnamese woman hugged him? *(His mother)*

3. Why do you think Huy was more afraid of the light-haired woman than Co Hai? *(Perhaps because the light-haired woman was different from him; because he had never seen anyone like her before; or because he believed the stories about her.)*

4. According to Co Hai, why did Huy bump into her on the dark street? *(Because God caused him to do so in answer to the women's prayer.)*

5. How did Huy get inside the large house? *(He lost consciousness and the light-haired woman carried him there.)*

6. Why did Huy suddenly stop eating his meal of fish and rice? *(He realized he had forgotten to offer some of his food to his Buddha.)*

7. Why do you think Co Hai did not try to stop Huy when he offered some of his food to his Buddha and, later, when he ran out of the house? *(She respected his right to make his own decisions. She also trusted God to change his heart someday and help him make the right decisions.)*

8. What were some of the things Co Hai said about Jesus? *(He is God's only Son; He taught great crowds and healed the sick; He loves all people; He died for sinners; God accepted His sacrifice and raised Him from the dead.)*

9. What did Co Hai show Huy that terrified him? Why did this scare him? *(Her black Book. He had been told that it was a book of magic, and he thought he had been trapped.)*

10. What did Co Hai do as soon as Huy left the house? *(She prayed that he would return and come to know God.)*

Chapter 3

1. Why did Huy consider returning to the children's home? *(He needed to get help for Kim, who was slowly starving to death.)*
2. What reasons did Huy have for not taking Kim to the children's home? *(He wasn't sure that they would care for her, since he had run away; he did not want to give her up; he was afraid she would worship the foreign God and make Buddha angry; he thought he could care for her himself.)*
3. What did Huy tell Co Hai that made her sad? *(He told her the lies he had heard about how her friend, the light-haired woman, harmed children.)*
4. How many people in this story were separated from his or her father and mother? *(Three: Huy, Kim, and the light-haired woman.)*
5. What did Huy say to Co Hai after he touched the Bible and nothing happened? Why do you think he said this? *(He said, "We are friends." He realized that he could trust her.)*
6. What things did Huy learn from the Bible? *(He learned about Heaven, sin, Jesus, and everlasting life.)*
7. How did Huy go from having a sinful heart to having a clean, pure heart? *(He asked Jesus to forgive his sins.)*
8. What caused Huy and those who cared for the children to become afraid? *(They learned that the Communist soldiers were coming to try to take their city.)*
9. What difficult decision did Huy have to make concerning Kim? *(Whether or not to allow Kim to be taken to the missionary's country)*
10. What do you think you would do if you were in Huy's place? *(Perhaps trust the missionary and let Kim go.)*

Chapter 4

1. Who helped Huy make the decision of whether or not to allow Kim to go to the missionary's country? *(The Holy Spirit)*
2. What did Huy mean by these words, "I love her [Kim] . . . enough to let her leave me"? *(He meant that he was willing to do what was best for her, even if it caused him pain.)*
3. What did Huy often think about as he was falling asleep? *(His mother– where she was and what she would think about the decisions he was making.)*
4. What was Huy's attitude like after Kim was gone? *(He was depressed and lonely. He wondered if Kim would forget all about him.)*
5. What exciting news did the two women share with Huy? *(That he would be allowed to go to the country where his sister lived)*
6. What did Huy pray in his heart when he realized that he had never thought about the missionary also having a sister whom she missed? *(He prayed that God would make him more unselfish.)*
7. As Huy was saying goodbye to Co Hai, what did she ask him to do for her? *(She asked him to pray for her.)*
8. What familiar voice did Huy hear while he was waiting to board the plane? *(His mother's voice)*
9. Why was Huy afraid to turn around when he heard the familiar voice? *(He was afraid that what he hoped for might not be true–that the voice might not be his mother's.)*
10. What had Huy's mother been doing since she escaped from the soldiers? *(She had been living with a kind family and searching for Huy and Kim.)*

Chapter 5

1. What question did Huy know that his mother wanted to ask? *(Was Kim all right?)*
2. How did Huy expect his mother to react when he told her that he no longer believed in Buddha? *(He expected she would be angry, since she had warned him to take care of the family idol.)*
3. How did his mother react when she heard about Huy's new beliefs, and why? *(She smiled because she now also believed in the living God, not Buddha.)*
4. What did Huy's mother hope would happen when Kim finally saw her again? *(She hoped that Kim would remember her and know she was her mother.)*
5. What were some of the things in the American airport that frightened Huy and the others from Vietnam? *(The great building, bright lights, white people, smells, and sounds.)*
6. What did Huy find unusual about the boys' bedroom where he slept? *(The boys slept on beds, instead of mats on the floor.)*
7. What were some of the strong and sometimes negative emotions Huy experienced in this story? *(Fear, loneliness, anger, grief)*
8. What were some of the positive emotions he experienced? *(Love, peace, joy, hope)*
9. Lying on his mat, Huy imagined how easy it would have been for the missionary to have never left her home. How might Huy's life have been different if she had never come to his land? *(He might never have heard about Jesus; he and Kim might have starved to death on the streets.)*
10. What promise did Huy make to God? *(He promised he would study hard and someday go wherever God sent him and share about the living God; and, in the meantime, that he would share with those he met in America.)*

www.ingramcontent.com/pod-product-compliance
Lightning Source LLC
Chambersburg PA
CBHW042018080426
42735CB00002B/92